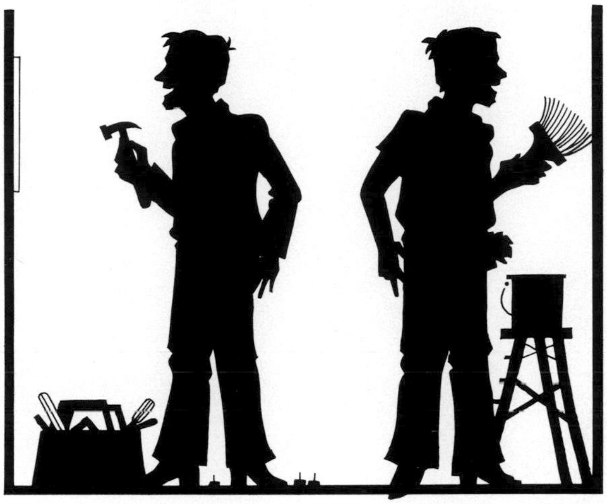

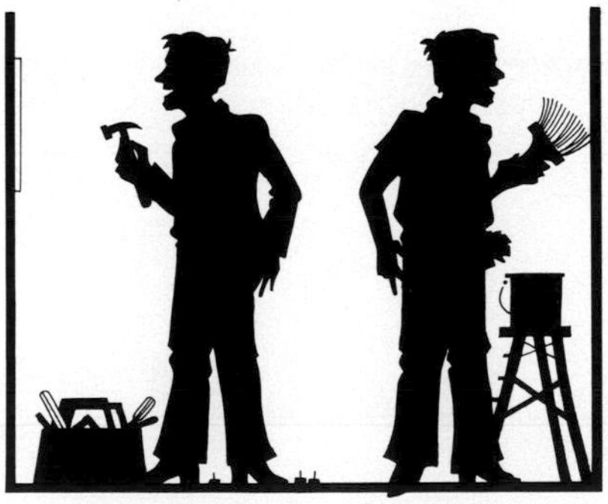

BUS

BUS

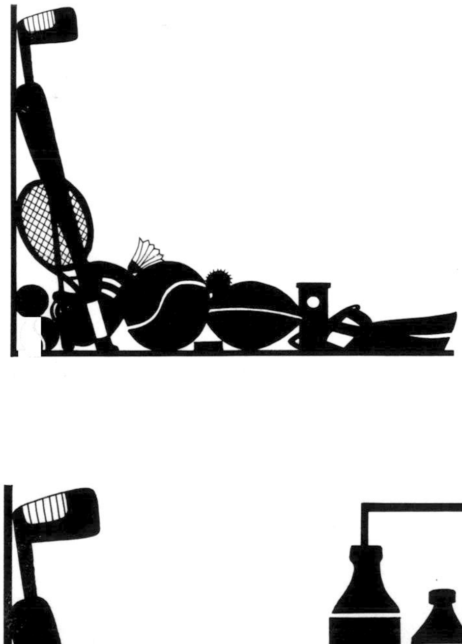

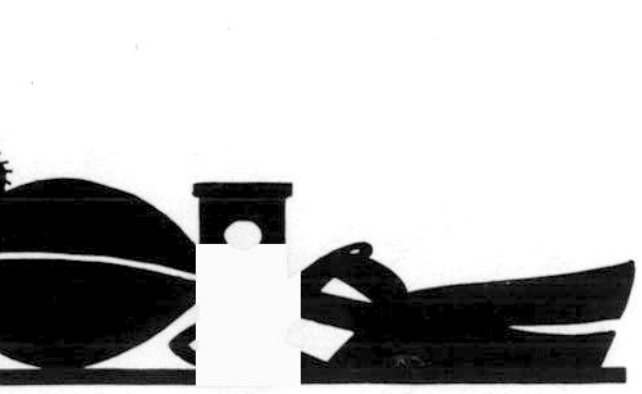

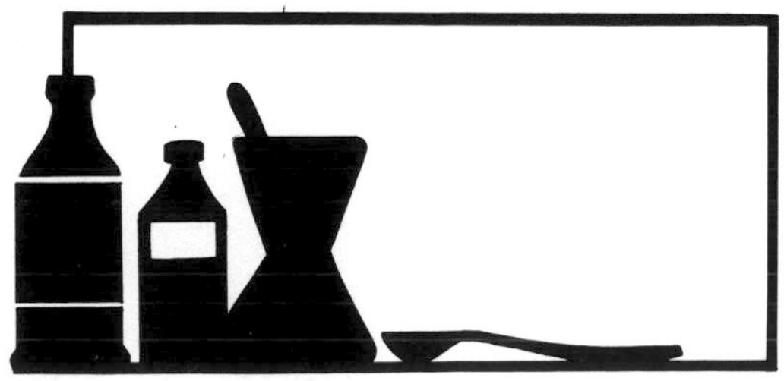

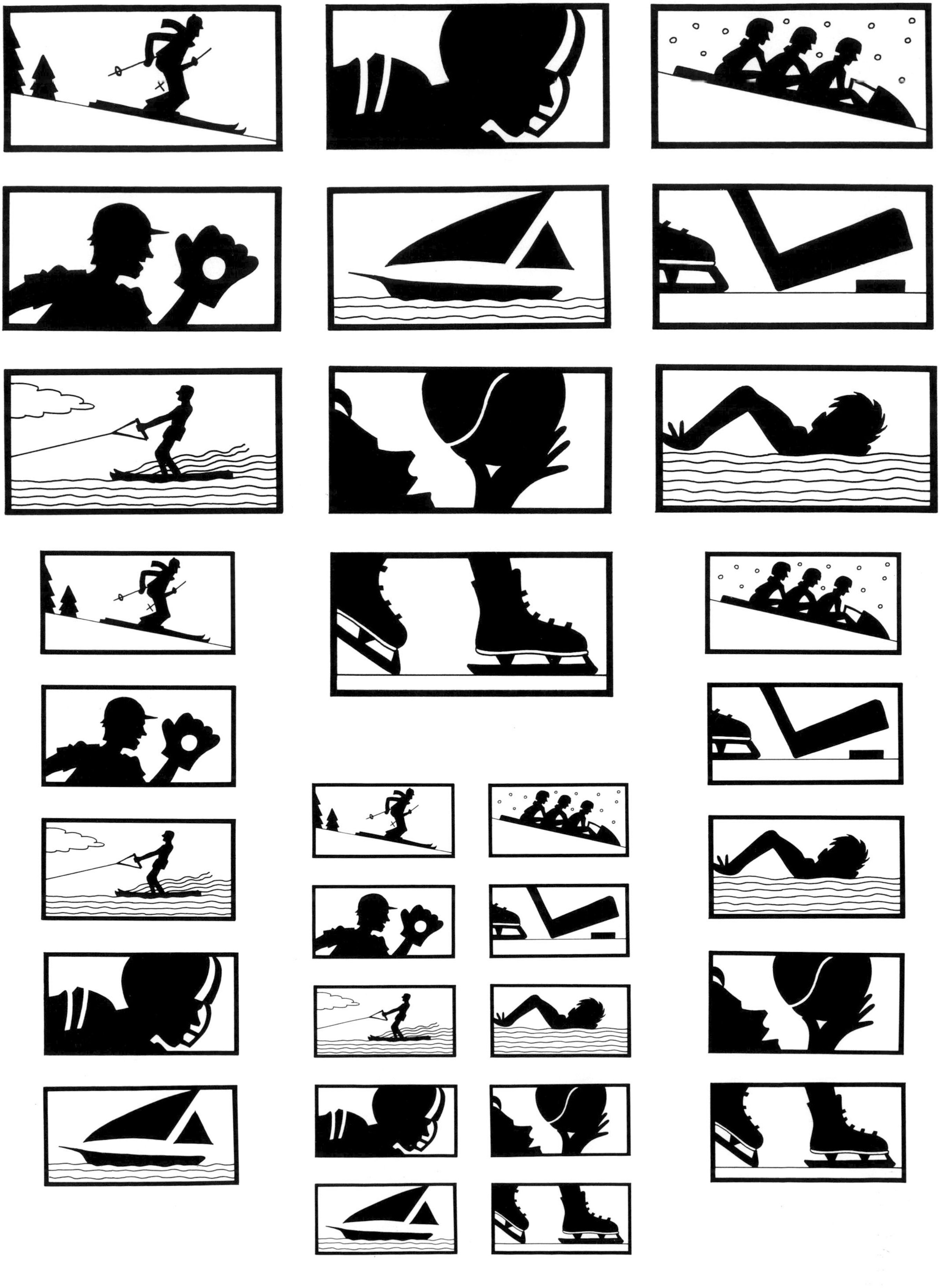

TICKET

TICKET

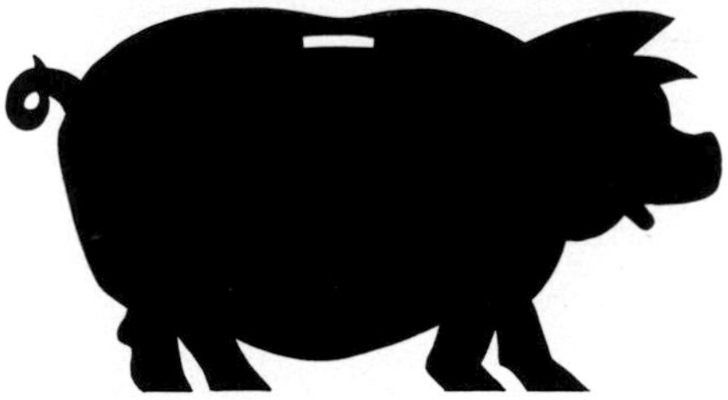

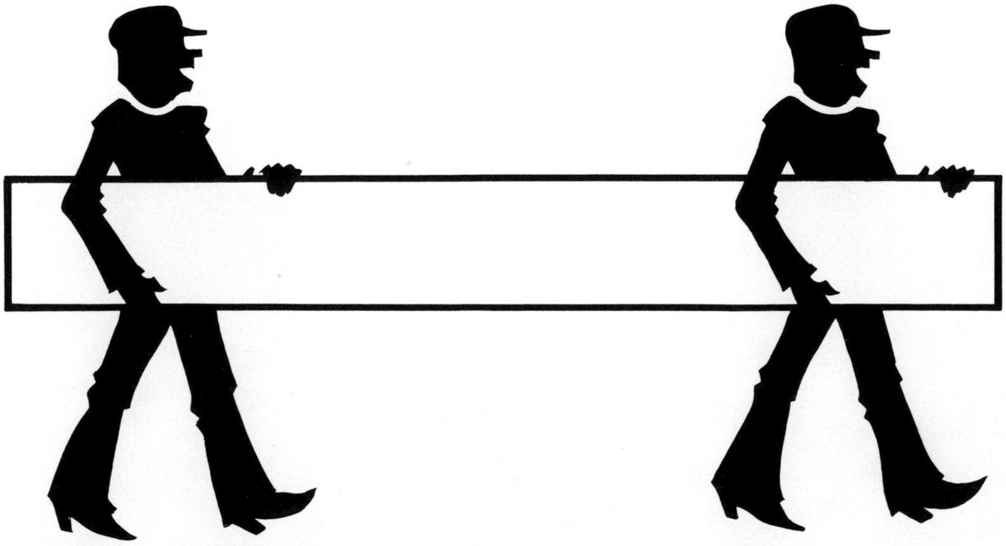

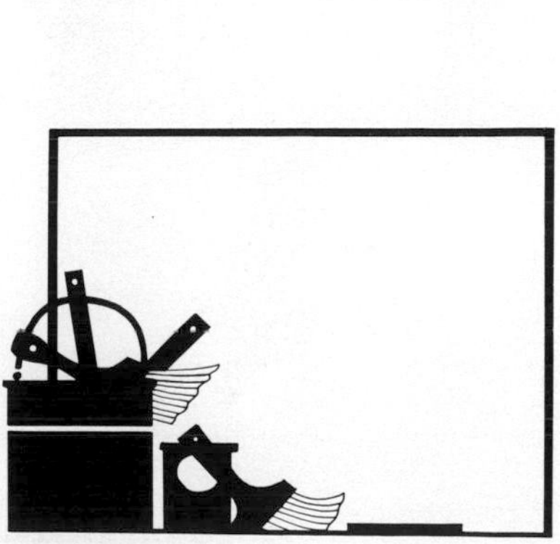

Repair Bill

Repair Bill